An Easy Way to Teach Reading to Beginners:

3 Fun Steps for Early Readers and ESL Students

Paul Smith

ISBN 10: 0-9831698-0-2

ISBN 13: 978-0-9831698-0-2

Published by: Expert Author Publishing

http://expertauthorpublishing.com

Canadian Address

1265 Charter Hill Drive

Coquitlam, BC, V3E 1P1

Phone: (604) 941-3041

Fax: (604) 944-7993

US Address

1300 Boblett Street

Unit A-218

Blaine, WA 98230

Phone: (866) 492-6623

Fax: (250) 493-6603

This is a simple, easy-to-use tool to get beginning readers off to a quick start. It is a system that is easy to learn and easy to teach. The method is highly visual, using pictures familiar to young children and new English language learners. Within days, sometimes within a single session, you can see progress. Students feel engaged and successful almost immediately doing something that makes sense to them. The manual also contains a scaffolded spelling program and several educational puzzles.

Paul Smith
paulsmithlac@yahoo.ca

"This is a very sensible and well-thought out series of activities to help children learn the alphabetical principle. I believe that it will help children learn some basic reading skills."

- Dr. Linda Siegel
Reading & Dyslexia Expert
UBC

Table of Contents

Section 1

Teaching Sight Words

(Use the pictures to make the sounds needed to read and decode the words.)

Work through 2-3 pages. Then have the student repeat those same pages until they have mastered them. It may work best if you master 1-4 pages at time depending on the student. Just keep repeating until the decoding becomes automatic.

At some point you can turn the page over to the words without pictures. The student can then read without the picture cues.

Teaching Notes:

A. It is often best to work in short sessions, 8-12 minutes.

B. The rhyming pattern of eeee-me, eee-she, eee-we can be useful in the beginning. When your student is able to recognize and produce the word without using the helping hand position, encourage them to just say the word itself. That is- me, she, we, etc.

Note: Unfortunately, due to the nature of the program it is necessary to use some pictures that do no match the spelling of the word. Ie. Earth/er, eye/I, cookie/ck etc.

Instructions:

Teacher note:

Starting with the vowel sound can build a useful rhyming pattern. This can help students learn quicker.
i.e.: "e-me, e-we, e-she, e-he, e-see"

me

Find the "helping hand" symbol.

②

me

Look at the picture above the "helping hand" symbol.

③

me

"ē"

Say the first sound of the picture that is indicated in the quotes below.

④

me

Point to the picture at the front of the word and say its first sound, "mmmmmm".

⑤

me

Slide your finger across the word, sounding it out, "mmmeeee"

"ē - me"

"ē - we"

"ē - she"

"ē - he"

"ē - see"

"be"

me	**we**
she	**he**
see	**be**

I

"I"

by

"I - by"

my

"I - my"

why

"I - why"

like

"I - like"

saw

"aw - saw"

on

"aw - on"

off

"aw - off"

10

I	by
my	why

like	

saw	

on	off

"un - run"

"un - sun"

"un - fun"

"un - done"

"uh - up"

"uh - us"

"uh - of"

"uh - was"

"uh - the"

run	sun
f un	d one
up	us
of	
was	the

come

"um - come"

some

"um - some"

from

"um - from"

gum

"um - gum"

jump

"um - jump"

tummy

"um - tummy"

sing

"ing - sing"

wing

"ing - wing"

ring

"ing - ring"

bring

"ing - bring"

come	some
from	gum
jump	tummy
sing	wing
ring	bring

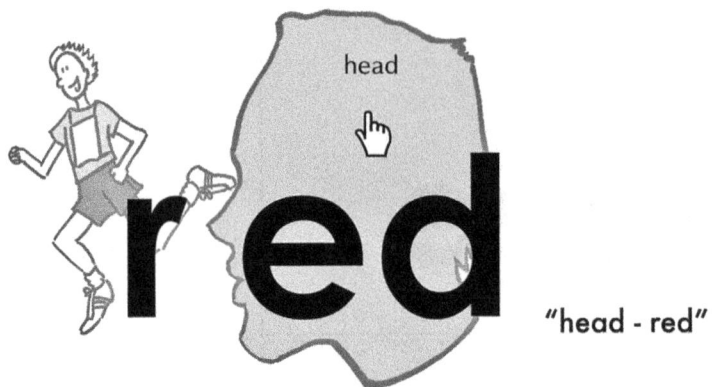

"head - red"

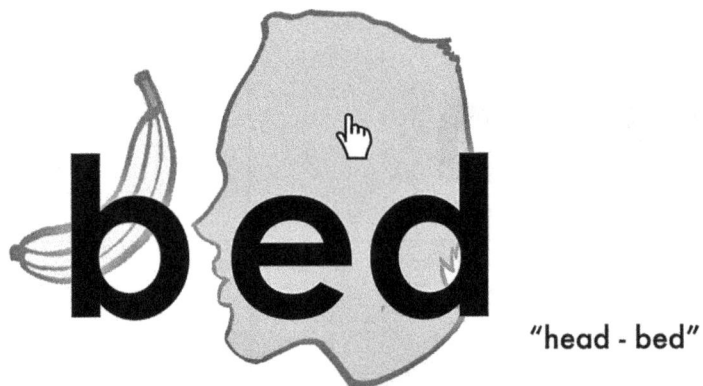

"head - bed"

"head - said"

"head - bread"

16

red

---

bed

---

said

---

bread

"hill"

"hill - will"

"hill - fill"

"hill - pill"

"hood - could"

"hood - would"

"hood - should"

"hood - good"

hill	will
fill	pill
could	would
should	good

 **for**
"or - for"

 **door**
"or - door"

 **your**
"or - your"

 **four**
"or - four"

 **more**
"or - more"

 **store**
"or - store"

 **or**
"or"

 **car**
"ar - car"

 **far**
"ar - far"

 **are**
"are"

 **her**
"er - her"

for	door	your
four		more
store		or
car		far
are		her

hula hoop

"who - to"

"who - do"

"who - you"

"who - zoo"

"who - new"

"who"

to	do
you	zoo
new	who

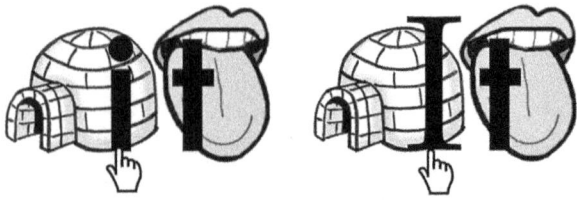 

"ĭ -It "   "ĭ -It "

"ĭ -Is "   "ĭ -Is "

"ĭ -If "

"in"

"hĭ - his"

"hĭ - him"

"oh - no"

"oh - go"

"oh - so"

"oh - show"

24

it	is
if	in
his	him
no	go
so	show

"er - her"

"er - girl"

"oy - boy"

"oy - toy"

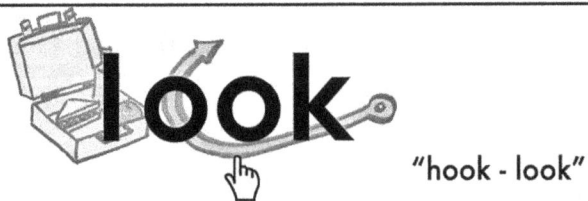

"hook - look"

26

her

girl

boy

toy

look

"look"

"took"

"look"

"look"

"put"

"look"

"look"

"push"

"look"

"look"

"pull"

"look"

look	took	look
look	put	look
look	push	look
look	pull	look

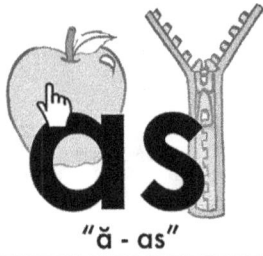
as
"ă - as"

at
"ă - at"

am
"ă - am"

has
"hă - has"

had
"hă - had"

have
"hă - have"

cat
"ă - cat"

man
"ăn - man"

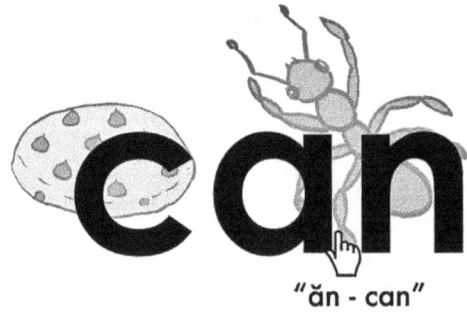
can
"ăn - can"

and
"ăn - and"

an
"ăn"

as	at	am
has		had
have		cat
man		can
and		an

tell
"el - tell"

well
"el - well"

help
"el - help"

men
"hen - men"

ten
"hen - ten"

went
"hen - went"

yes
"s - yes"

use
"zzz - use"

say
"hay - say"

may
"hay - may"

day
"hay - day"

play
"hay - play"

tell	well	help
men	ten	went

yes	use
say	may
day	play

then

"hen - then"

them

empty

"em- them"

they

"hay - they"

the

"uh - the"

there

"hair - there"

where

"hair - where"

when

"hen - when"

then	them
they	the
there	where

when

chair

"hair - chair"

bear

"hair - bear"

fair

"hair - fair"

care

"hair - care"

ear

"ear"

here

"ear - here"

deer

"ear - deer"

chair	bear
fair	care
ear	here

deer

cow

"ow - cow"

now

"ow - now"

wow

"ow - wow"

how

"ow - how"

out

"ow - out"

ball

"hall - ball"

call

"hall - call"

tall

"hall - tall"

wall

"hall - wall"

cow	now
wow	how

out

ball	call
tall	wall

 **came**

"hay - came"

 **name**

"hay - name"

 **make**

"hay - make"

 **game**

"hay - game"

 **made**

"hay - made"

 **cake**

"hay - cake"

 **take**

"hay - take"

 **gave**

"hay - gave"

 **baby**

"hay - baby"

came	name	make
game	made	cake
take	gave	baby

"I"

"I - time"

"I - five"

"I - nine"

"I - hide"

"I - fire"

"I - light"

"I - night"

"I - right"

"eye"

I	time
five	nine
hide	fire
light	night
right	eye

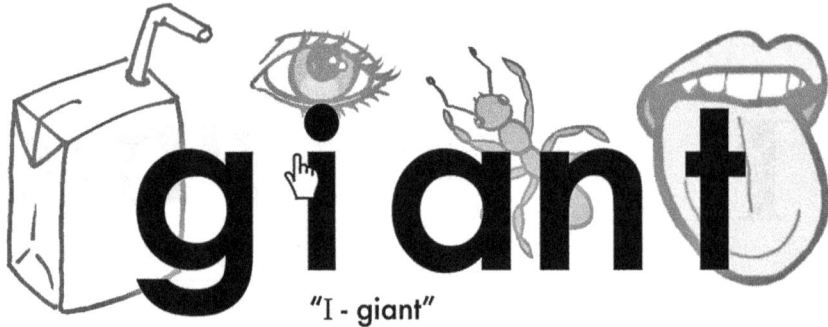

"I - giant"

"I - climb"

"I - my"

"I - by"

"I - try"

"I - fly"

giant

climb

my	by
try	fly

 **rose** "oh - rose"

 **old** "oh - old"

 **cold** "oh - cold"

 **those** "oh - those"

 **know** "oh - know"

46

rose

old

cold

those

know

 **bought**   *"aw - bought"*

 **brought**   *"aw - brought"*

 **caught**   *"aw - caught"*

 **cough**   *"aw - cough"*

 **laugh**   *"ă - laugh"*

bought

---

brought

---

caught

---

cough

---

laugh

were

"er - were"

her

"er - her"

our

"er - our"

bird

"er - bird"

girl

"er - girl"

burn

"er - burn"

turn

"er - turn"

under

"er - under"

after

"er - after"

were	her
our	
bird	girl
burn	turn
under	
after	

Section 2

Spelling Program
Worksheets

(The worksheets are reproducible and meant to be used for repeated practice. If you are unable to make copies, leave the master blank and have the student place their answers on a separate piece of scrap paper.)

The following 24 worksheets can be used to scaffold your student through beginning spelling. As the student attempts to fill in the worksheets, you will be able to guide them as they start to sound out words. Some worksheets have prompts and letters at the top of the page to help your student identify the missing sounds.

Simply by having your student copy or fill in the worksheets repeatedly gives them valuable practice for spelling. The more automatic these sounds become the easier it is for the student to 'sound out' a word and spell it.

You may find most students like doing these sheets over and over. They enjoy the familiarity of the task and it helps build their confidence when they see their own progress. Rote learning can be very effective in acquiring new skills. They should be able to increase their speed as they continue to practice these drills.

As the student masters one sheet you can move them to the next or use the sheets in any order to reinforce previous learning.

Again, you will want the sounds in the worksheets to become automatic. It is therefore necessary to do these sheets over and over. For students who need extra support, allow them to copy answers. You can fill in any of the spelling sheets and have them copy for practice.
Practice. Practice. Practice.

Note: It is also important to have your students generate their own writing. Have them write a sentence or two using the sounds they know. There are many creative and meaningful ways you can have your student write. For example, they could keep a diary, make a to-do list or write a message to someone.

1 letter color red	**1 letter** color red	**1 letter** color red
1 letter color red	**blends/decoding 2-3 letters** color orange	**blends/decoding 2-3 letters** color orange
blends/decoding 2-3 letters color orange	**blends/decoding 2-3 letters** color orange	**blends/decoding 2-3 letters** color orange
blends/decoding 2-3 letters color orange	**blends/decoding 2-3 letters** color orange	**diagraphs/ vowel sounds** color yellow
diagraphs/ vowel sounds color yellow	**diagraphs/ vowel sounds** color yellow	**diagraphs/ vowel sounds** color green
diagraphs/ vowel sounds color green	**diagraphs/ vowel sounds** color green	**diagraphs/ vowel sounds** color green
diagraphs/ vowel sounds color green	**hard/soft sounds silent letters, controlled r, ed, magic e** color green	**sight words** color green
sight words color green	Copy, color, and cut these rectangles for organizing your supply of practice sheets.	

53

Vowels and consonants 1

a — (alien)	e —	i —	o — (ocean)	u —
a —	e — (everyone)	i —	o —	u — (up)
m —	s —	f —	t —	h —
d —	j — (juice box)	v —	n —	k —
b —	l —	p —	w —	c —
r —	y —	z —	g —	qu —

Vowels and consonants 1   Red 1

a b c d e f g h i j k l m n o p q r s t u v w x y z

___ alien	___	___	___ ocean	___
___	___ everyone	___	___	___ up
___	___	___	___	___
___	___ juice box	___	___	___
___	___	___	___	___
___	___	___	___	___

Vowels and consonants 2

d	s	f	m	t
h	j	v	n	k
b	l	w	c	r
y yogurt	z	g	qu	i
a	o	e everyone	U up	o ocean
i	a alien	e	U	p

56

Vowels and consonants 2   Red 2

a b c d e f g h i j k l m n o p q r s t u v w x y z

___	___ STOP	___	___	___
___	___	___	___	___
___	___	___	___	___
___ yogurt	___	___	___	___
___	___	___ everyone	___ up	___ ocean
___	___ alien	___	___	___

57

Vowel Practice - long and short **aeiou** ^{Red}

___	___ everyone	___	___	___ up
___ alien	___	___	ocean ___	___
___	___	___	___	___
___	___	___	___	___
___	___	___	___	___
___	___	___	___	___

58

Tricky Consonant Practice What do you hear? **n l r h d**   Red

Orange
a e i o u

Consonant plus a vowel 1: What vowel do you hear?

_ _ atballs	_ _ se	_ _ at	_ _ rate	_ _ ght
_ _ dybug	_ _ inting	_ _ _ -saw	_ _ il	_ _ _ e
_ _ ne	_ _ by	_ _ bra	_ _ bot	_ _ ke
_ _ ke	_ _ _ _ -saw	_ _ eth	_ _ ble	_ _ _ on
_ _ ys	_ _ ien	_ _ _ _	_ _ _ olin	_ _ ap
_ _ _ _ t	_ _ inbow	_ _ ading	candy _ _ _ ne	_ _ ilbox

60

Orange
a e i o u

Consonant plus a vowel 2: What vowel do you hear?

_ _ _ -saw	_ _ atballs	_ _ eth	_ _ bot	_ _ on
_ _ _ _	_ _ at	_ _ bra	_ _ ap	_ _ ke
_ _ _ t	_ _ ve	_ _ ke	_ _ ble	_ _ ilbox
_ _ by	_ _ _ _ dy _ _ _ _ e	_ _ t	_ _	_ _ t
_ _ eryone	_ _ loo	_ _ sh	_ _ bbit rabbit	_ _ g
_ _ ps	_ _ d	_ _ t	_ _ g	_ _ ppo

61

Orange
a e i o u

Consonant plus a vowel 3: What vowel do you hear?

_ _ e	_ _ ien	_ _ _ dy _ e	_ _ il	_ _ ght
_ _ dybug	_ _ inting	_ _ ading	_ _ gurt	_ _ se
_ _ ne 9	_ _ _ le	_ _ th	_ _ cuum	_ _ stle
_ _ mmer	_ _ dder	_ _ ncil	_ _ n 10	_ _ mon
_ _ ven 7	_ _ pper	_ _ x 6	_ _ ck	_ _ x
_ _ n	_ _ n	_ _ tterfly	_ _ _ -saw	_ _ atballs

Orange

Blends Practice 1: Can you hear? **l r n t**

_ unch	_ _ ower	_ _ ock	_ unch	_ _ ide
_ _ ant	_ unch	_ _ ue	_ _ ocks	_ umbers
_ _ ake	_ ongue	_ _ ar	_ _ _ _ aw	_ un
_ _ og	_ _ ead	_ _ apes	_ un	_ _ incess
_ _ ayons	_ _ ee	_ _ ess	_ _ ider	_ _ ile
_ _ ins	_ _ arf	_ _ ing	_ _ ate	_ _ agon

Orange

Blends Practice 2: Can you hear? **l r n t**

_ un	_ _ ince	_ _ oom	_ _ ass	_ un
_ _ ies	_ _ y	_ _ ain	_ _ agon	_ unch
_ _ ag	_ _ oud	_ unch	_ _ eep	_ _ ane
_ unch	_ _ asses	_ _ ueberries	_ umbers	_ _ ail
_ ongue	_ _ op	_ _ _ eet	_ _ oon	_ _ ell
_ _ im	_ _ ip	_ _ arecrow	_ _ elve	_ _ ess

64

Consonant-Vowel-Consonant Practice
What vowel do you hear?

_ _ _ ot	_ _ _ ybug	_ _ _ le	_ _ _ ra	_ _ _ _
_ _ _ lin	_ _ _ y	_ _ _ e	_ _ _ e	_ _ _ -saw
_ _ atballs	_ _ _ urt	_ _ _ e	_ _ _ t	_ _ _ terfly
_ _ _ mer	_ _ _	_ _ _ s	_ _ _ _	_ _
_ _ _ uum	_ _ _	_ _ _ _ er	_ _ _ tle	_ _ _ _ _ aur
_ _ _	_ _ _ _	_ _ _ _	_ _ _ _	_ _ _ po

65

Orange

Blends Practice 3: Can you hear? **l r n t**

_ _ _ te	_ _ _ le	_ _ _der	_ _ _	_ _ _ ck
_ _ _ de	_ _ _ cks	_ _ _ ke	_ _ _ g	_ _ _ pes
_ _ _ _	_ _ _ _	_ _ _ ss	_ _ _ yons	_ _ _ ss
_ _ e	_ _ _ _	_ _ _ m	_ _ _ p	_ _ _ _ p
_ _ _ in	_ _ _ ne	_ _ _	_ _ _ sses	_ _ _ il
_ _ _ p	_ _ _ _ _ t	_ _ atballs	_ _ _ _	_ _

66

Digraph practice - 2 letters make 1 sound
What do you hear?

yellow
ch wh sh th - tr dr

_ ouse	_ un	_ _ uck	_ _ air	_ _ ain
_ _ ess	_ _ oe	_ _ eel	_ _ ere	_ _ agon
_ ouse	_ _ eckers	_ _ ee	_ _ umb	_ _ ale
_ un	_ _ ess	_ _ ark	_ _ air	_ _ agon
_ _ ale	_ _ ell	_ _ ain	_ _ ale	_ _ eckers
_ _ uck	_ _ eel	_ _ oe	_ _ ere	_ _ ess

The pictures are used to show the sound being indicated and do not necessarily match the spelling.
Some squares show different combinations of letters that spell the same sound. For example: e, ee and ea all
spell the long vowel sound e (me, see and tea) (er, ir and ur - her, fir and fur) (i, igh - hi and high)

Digraphs/vowel sounds

yellow
Student copies sounds

ā / āy / āi	ē / ēē / ēa	ī / īgh	ō / ōa	ū
alien			ocean	
s̄h̄	c̄h̄	t̄h̄ (there) / t̄h̄	w̄h̄	c̄ / k̄ / c̄k̄
ēr / īr / ūr earth	ōr	ār	h__ āir	ēar / ēēr
h__k ōō	ōy / ōi oil	ōw / ōū	__t h̄ā	__ppo h̄ī
ā n̄t	ī n̄	h__ ēn̄	ēT	ēm empty
ūn̄ under	ūm̄	h__ āTT	h__ īTT	k___ īng

68

yellow

Digraphs/vowel sounds

— — — — — alien	— — —	— — — —	— — — ocean	—
— —	— —	— — there	— —	— — — —
		— —	— —	
— — — — — — earth	— —	— —	h _ _ _	— — — — — —
h _ _ k	— — — —	— — — — oil	_ _ t	_ _ ppo
_ _ t	— —	h _ _	— —	— — empty
— — under	— —	h _ _ _	h _ _ _	k _ _ _

69

green

What sounds are missing?

c _ _	_ _ eese	m _ _	w _ _ dow	b _ d	b _ _ l
p _ g	f _ _ t	w _ _ _	p _ _ cil	_ _ ale	_ _ _
du _ _	d _ g	dr _ _	l _ _ on	c _ _	c _ p
_ _ umb	h _ _ _	c _ t	p _ _ _ ow	_ _ t	l _ _ _ t
b _ _ k	b _ _ _ _	f _ ve	h _ _ se	c _ ke	rul _ _
_ _ ark	_ _ one	s _ _	b _ ne	_ _ ere	b _ _

green

What sounds are missing?

__ell	h____	dr__	br__n m__se	t__ 10	sn__ __l
w____	__eckers	l__on	r_t	d____	st__
__iskers	p__	h_t d_g	h__icopter	r__	__oto
br_ad	s__p	r____	bla__ tru__	__ppy	h__d
st__e	__ere	b_ke	ba__	t__s	c__k
n_ts	n____t	gr__n t__	st____s	l_ps	m____maid

PHOTOCOPY

green

What sounds are missing?

	e			
_ _ _	_ _ _ e	_ _ _	_ _ _	_ _ _
_ _ _ _ _ _			_ _ _ e	
_ _ _	_ _ _ e	_ _ _	_ _ _	_ _ _
_ _ _ cess	_ _ _	_ _ _	_ _ _	_ _ _
_ _ _	_ _ _ es	_ _ _ e	_ _ _	_ _ _
_ _ _	_ _ _	_ _ _	_ _ _	_ _ _ aw

72

green

What sounds are missing?

____se	____	____	____ow	____	____
____	____	w____	____cil	___le	____
____	____	____	____on	____	____
____b	____	____	____ow	____	____
____	____	____e	____e	___e	rul__
____	____e	____	____e	__ere	____

green

What sounds are missing?

			___ ___ ___ e	___ ___ ___	___ ___ ___ l
w ___ ___ ___	___ ___ ckers	___ ___ ___ on	___ ___ ___	___ ___ ___	___ ___ ___
___iskers	___ ___ ___	___ ___ ___	___ ___ icopter	___ ___ ___	___ ___ ___
___ ___ ___	___ ___ ___	___ ___ ___	___ ___ ___	___ ___ ___ y	___ ___ ___
___ ___ e	___ ere	___ ___ e	___ ___ ___ ___	___ ___ ___	___ ___ ___
___ ___ ___	___ ___ ___	___ ___ ___	___ ___ ___ s	___ ___ ___	___ ___ aid

74

Hard and soft letters

green

hard	soft

c _ at

c _ ircle

g _ host

g _ iant

Silent letters

kn	mb
_ _ ife	thu_ _
_ _ ees	co_ _

Controlled r er-ir-ur

There are 3 ways to spell the 'er' sound.

rul_ _   g_ _ l   p_ _ se

m_ _ maid   b_ _ d   ch_ _ ch

The 'ed' sound at the end of a word can have a 't' or a 'd' sound   **ed**   **ed**

jump_ _   push_ _   pull_ _

magic e   a → a   an "e" on the end of a word can change the vowel sound from short to long

t_ p   t_ p_

75

green

Sight words   student copies words

_ _ _
who

_ _ _ _
he   him
_ _ _ _
she   her
_ _ _ _ _ _ _ _
they   them

_ _ _ _
what ?

_ _ _ _ _ _ _ _
this   that
_ _ _ _ _ _ _ _ _ _
these   those

_ _ _ _ _
where

_ _ _ _ _
there

_ _ _ _
when

_ _ _ _
then

_ _ _
why

_ _ _ _ _ _ _
because

"We went swimming", said the children .

"I want to go for a walk", said the dog .

76

green

Sight words

— — — —

— — — — — (?)

— — — — —

— — — —

— — —
y

— — — — —
b

Section 3 - Puzzles

Make your own fun puzzles

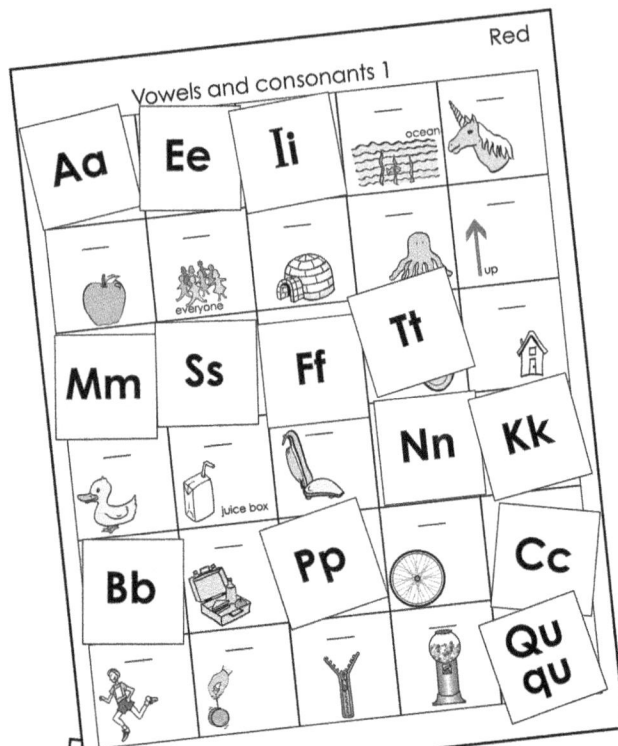

Red

Vowels and consonants 1

Aa	Ee	Ii	ocean	unicorn
apple	everyone	igloo		up
Mm	Ss	Ff	Tt	house
duck	juice box		Nn	Kk
Bb		Pp		Cc
				Qu qu

C

The | robot | is | on | the | yoyo | .

The | zipper | is | on | the | gum | .
color this line red

The | queen | is | on | the | duck | .
color this line light green

The | flower | is | on | the | clock | .
color this line light orange

The | slide | is | on | the | plant | .
color this line yellow

C

I | like | the | robot | and | the | yoyo | .
color this line light blue

I | like | the | zipper | and | the | gum | .
color this line pink

I | like | the | queen | and | the | duck | .
color this line light green

I | like | the | flower | and | the | clock | .
color this line light orange

I | like | the | slide | and | the | plant | .
color this line yellow

Section 3

Puzzles – hands-on activities
(You can use a cookie sheet and magnetic tape to create puzzle pieces that your student can use over and over.)

You can create several puzzles in the manual.

A: Several of the worksheets can be turned into puzzles (pp. 54-77). Simply cut out the answers provided here and create puzzle pieces to be used with the worksheets.

B: There are also puzzles for sentence construction.
(Make sure to color-code according to the instructions. Without color-coding the puzzles would be far too difficult for a beginning reader.)

Coloring tip:
Use highlighters to color lines & puzzle pieces for best results.

Teaching Notes:
A: You may want to provide the student with a master copy. (photocopy the puzzle, then print the answers) In the beginning stages, students may need to see the answers in order to reproduce them.

B: You may also want to use the sentence puzzle as a worksheet.   Photocopy the puzzle and have students print the sentences.

C: You may want to use some different colored paper for the letter puzzles (pp. 54-77). It is easier to organize your puzzles and the students like the variety. Also, students can then work next to each other without getting their puzzle pieces mixed up.

A

everyone

color this line light blue

color this line pink

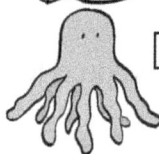

color this line light green

color this line light orange

color this line yellow

Puzzle A pieces option 1

I like the apple and everyone .

Color these rectangle pieces light blue and cut them out for your puzzle pieces.

I like the igloo and the octopus .

Color these rectangle pieces pink and cut them out for your puzzle pieces.

I like the umbrella and the monkey .

Color these rectangle pieces light green and cut them out for your puzzle pieces.

I like the sun and the fish .

Color these rectangle pieces light orange and cut them out for your puzzle pieces.

I like the tongue and the house .

Color these rectangle pieces yellow and cut them out for your puzzle pieces.

Puzzle A pieces option 2

| The | apple | is | on | everyone | . |

Color these rectangle pieces light blue and cut them out for your puzzle pieces.

| The | igloo | is | on | the | octopus | . |

Color these rectangle pieces pink and cut them out for your puzzle pieces.

| The | umbrella | is | on | the | monkey | . |

Color these rectangle pieces light green and cut them out for your puzzle pieces.

| The | sun | is | on | the | fish | . |

Color these rectangle pieces light orange and cut them out for your puzzle pieces.

| The | tongue | is | on | the | house | . |

Color these rectangle pieces yellow and cut them out for your puzzle pieces.

B

color this line light blue

color this line pink

color this line light green

color this line light orange

color this line yellow

Puzzle B pieces option 1

I | like | the | juice | and | the | house | .

Color these rectangle pieces light blue and cut them out for your puzzle pieces.

I | like | the | vacuum | and | the | nuts | .

Color these rectangle pieces pink and cut them out for your puzzle pieces.

I | like | the | king | and | the | banana | .

Color these rectangle pieces light green and cut them out for your puzzle pieces.

I | like | the | lunch | and | the | pig | .

Color these rectangle pieces light orange and cut them out for your puzzle pieces.

I | like | the | wheel | and | the | cookie | .

Color these rectangle pieces yellow and cut them out for your puzzle pieces.

Puzzle B pieces option 2

The | juice | is | on | the | house | .

Color these rectangle pieces light blue and cut them out for your puzzle pieces.

The | vacuum | is | on | the | nuts | .

Color these rectangle pieces pink and cut them out for your puzzle pieces.

The | king | is | on | the | banana | .

Color these rectangle pieces light green and cut them out for your puzzle pieces.

The | lunch | is | on | the | pig | .

Color these rectangle pieces light orange and cut them out for your puzzle pieces.

The | wheel | is | on | the | cookie | .

Color these rectangle pieces yellow and cut them out for your puzzle pieces.

C

color this line light blue

color this line pink

color this line light green

color this line light orange

color this line yellow

Puzzle C pieces option 1

I like the robot and the yoyo .

Color these rectangle pieces light blue and cut them out for your puzzle pieces.

I like the zipper and the ghost .

Color these rectangle pieces pink and cut them out for your puzzle pieces.

I like the queen and the duck .

Color these rectangle pieces light green and cut them out for your puzzle pieces.

I like the flower and the clock .

Color these rectangle pieces light orange and cut them out for your puzzle pieces.

I like the slide and the plant .

Color these rectangle pieces yellow and cut them out for your puzzle pieces.

Puzzle C pieces option 2

The | robot | is | on | the | yoyo | .

Color these rectangle pieces light blue and cut them out for your puzzle pieces.

The | zipper | is | on | the | ghost | .

Color these rectangle pieces pink and cut them out for your puzzle pieces.

The | queen | is | on | the | duck | .

Color these rectangle pieces light green and cut them out for your puzzle pieces.

The | flower | is | on | the | clock | .

Color these rectangle pieces light orange and cut them out for your puzzle pieces.

The | slide | is | on | the | plant | .

Color these rectangle pieces yellow and cut them out for your puzzle pieces.

D

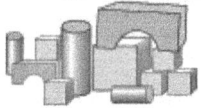

color this line light blue

color this line pink

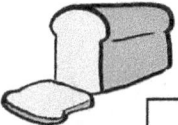

twins

color this line light green

color this line light orange

color this line yellow

Puzzle D pieces option 1

I like the glue and the blocks .

Color these rectangle pieces light blue and cut them out for your puzzle pieces.

I like the spider and the twins .

Color these rectangle pieces pink and cut them out for your puzzle pieces.

I like the bread and the grapes .

Color these rectangle pieces light green and cut them out for your puzzle pieces.

I like the tree and the dress .

Color these rectangle pieces light orange and cut them out for your puzzle pieces.

I like the princess and the crayons .

Color these rectangle pieces yellow and cut them out for your puzzle pieces.

Puzzle D pieces option 2

The | glue | is | on | the | blocks | .

Color these rectangle pieces light blue and cut them out for your puzzle pieces.

The | spider | is | on | the | twins | .

Color these rectangle pieces pink and cut them out for your puzzle pieces.

The | bread | is | on | the | grapes | .

Color these rectangle pieces light green and cut them out for your puzzle pieces.

The | tree | is | on | the | dress | .

Color these rectangle pieces light orange and cut them out for your puzzle pieces.

The | princess | is | on | the | crayons | .

Color these rectangle pieces yellow and cut them out for your puzzle pieces.

E

color this line light blue

color this line pink

color this line light green

color this line light orange

color this line yellow

Puzzle E pieces option 1

I like the alien and the eagle . ✂

Color these rectangle pieces light blue and cut them out for your puzzle pieces.

I like the ocean and the unicorn . ✂

Color these rectangle pieces pink and cut them out for your puzzle pieces.

I like the apple and everyone . ✂

Color these rectangle pieces light green and cut them out for your puzzle pieces.

I like the igloo and the alien . ✂

Color these rectangle pieces light orange and cut them out for your puzzle pieces.

I like the eagle and the igloo . ✂

Color these rectangle pieces yellow and cut them out for your puzzle pieces.

Puzzle E pieces option 2

The | alien | is | on | the | eagle | .

Color these rectangle pieces light blue and cut them out for your puzzle pieces.

The | ocean | is | on | the | unicorn | .

Color these rectangle pieces pink and cut them out for your puzzle pieces.

The | apple | is | on | everyone | .

Color these rectangle pieces light green and cut them out for your puzzle pieces.

The | igloo | is | on | the | alien | .

Color these rectangle pieces light orange and cut them out for your puzzle pieces.

The | eagle | is | on | the | igloo | .

Color these rectangle pieces yellow and cut them out for your puzzle pieces.

F

color this line light blue

color this line pink

color this line light green

color this line light orange

color this line yellow

color this line light purple

Puzzle F

| It | is | a | big | robot | . |

Color these rectangle pieces light blue and cut them out for your puzzle pieces.

| It | has | two | legs | . |

Color these rectangle pieces pink and cut them out for your puzzle pieces.

| It | is | a | little | cat | . |

Color these rectangle pieces light green and cut them out for your puzzle pieces.

| It | has | four | legs | . |

Color these rectangle pieces light orange and cut them out for your puzzle pieces.

| It | is | a | big | spider | . |

Color these rectangle pieces yellow and cut them out for your puzzle pieces.

| It | has | eight | legs | . |

Color these rectangle pieces light purple and cut them out for your puzzle pieces.

G

| color this line light blue |
| color this line pink |

| color this line light green |
| color this line light orange |

| color this line yellow |
| color this line light purple |

Puzzle G

It is a big cookie .

Color these rectangle pieces light blue and cut them out for your puzzle pieces.

You can eat it .

Color these rectangle pieces pink and cut them out for your puzzle pieces.

It is a little milk .

Color these rectangle pieces light green and cut them out for your puzzle pieces.

You can drink it .

Color these rectangle pieces light orange and cut them out for your puzzle pieces.

It is a big hat .

Color these rectangle pieces yellow and cut them out for your puzzle pieces.

You can wear it .

Color these rectangle pieces light purple and cut them out for your puzzle pieces.

H

color this line light blue

color this line pink

color this line light green

color this line light orange

color this line yellow

color this line light purple

Puzzle H

It | is | a | big | zebra | .

Color these rectangle pieces light blue and cut them out for your puzzle pieces.

It | is | black | and | white | .

Color these rectangle pieces pink and cut them out for your puzzle pieces.

It | is | a | little | bee | .

Color these rectangle pieces light green and cut them out for your puzzle pieces.

It | is | yellow | and | black | .

Color these rectangle pieces light orange and cut them out for your puzzle pieces.

It | is | a | big | tree | .

Color these rectangle pieces yellow and cut them out for your puzzle pieces.

It | is | green | and | brown | .

Color these rectangle pieces light purple and cut them out for your puzzle pieces.

I

color this line light blue

color this line pink

color this line light green

color this line light orange

color this line yellow

color this line light purple

I

Old MacDonald had a farm eieio .

Color these rectangle pieces light blue and cut them out for your puzzle pieces.

And on his farm he had a cow eieio .

Color these rectangle pieces pink and cut them out for your puzzle pieces.

The itsy bitsy spider went up the water spout .

Color these rectangle pieces light green and cut them out for your puzzle pieces.

Down came the rain and washed the spider out.

Color these rectangle pieces light orange and cut them out for your puzzle pieces.

Twinkle twinkle little star .

Color these rectangle pieces yellow and cut them out for your puzzle pieces.

How I wonder what you are .

Color these rectangle pieces light purple and cut them out for your puzzle pieces.

J

color this line light blue

color this line pink

color this line light green

color this line light orange

color this line yellow

color this line light purple

103

Puzzle J pieces

Happy | birthday | to | you | happy | birthday | to | you | . ✂

Color these rectangle pieces light blue and cut them out for your puzzle pieces.

Row | row | row | your | boat | gently | down | the | stream | . ✂

Color these rectangle pieces pink and cut them out for your puzzle pieces.

The | wheels | on | the | bus | go | round | and | round | . ✂

Color these rectangle pieces light green and cut them out for your puzzle pieces.

If | you're | happy | and | you | know | it | clap | your | hands | . ✂

Color these rectangle pieces light orange and cut them out for your puzzle pieces.

Rudolph | the | red | nose | reindeer | had | a | very | shiny | nose | . ✂

Color these rectangle pieces yellow and cut them out for your puzzle pieces.

Jingle | bells | jingle | bells | jingle | all | the | way | . ✂

Color these rectangle pieces light purple and cut them out for your puzzle pieces.

K

color this line light blue

color this line pink

color this line light green

color this line light orange

color this line yellow

Puzzle K pieces option 1

I like the cat and the pig . ✂

Color these rectangle pieces light blue and cut them out for your puzzle pieces.

I like the dog and the cat . ✂

Color these rectangle pieces pink and cut them out for your puzzle pieces.

I like the pig and the box . ✂

Color these rectangle pieces light green and cut them out for your puzzle pieces.

I like the cat and the box . ✂

Color these rectangle pieces light orange and cut them out for your puzzle pieces.

I like the pig and the hat . ✂

Color these rectangle pieces yellow and cut them out for your puzzle pieces.

PHOTOCOPY

Puzzle K pieces option 2

The | cat | is | on | the | pig | .

Color these rectangle pieces light blue and cut them out for your puzzle pieces.

The | dog | is | on | the | cat | .

Color these rectangle pieces pink and cut them out for your puzzle pieces.

The | pig | is | on | the | box | .

Color these rectangle pieces light green and cut them out for your puzzle pieces.

The | cat | is | on | the | box | .

Color these rectangle pieces light orange and cut them out for your puzzle pieces.

The | pig | is | on | the | hat | .

Color these rectangle pieces yellow and cut them out for your puzzle pieces.

107

color this line light blue

color this line pink

color this line light green

color this line light orange

Puzzle L pieces

The | pig | is | on | the | box | . ✂

Color these rectangle pieces light blue and cut them out for your puzzle pieces.

The | cat | is | on | the | box | . ✂

Color these rectangle pieces pink and cut them out for your puzzle pieces.

The | dog | is | on | the | box | . ✂

Color these rectangle pieces light green and cut them out for your puzzle pieces.

The | hat | is | on | the | box | . ✂

Color these rectangle pieces light orange and cut them out for your puzzle pieces.

M

color this line light blue

color this line pink

color this line light green

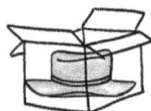

color this line light orange

Puzzle M pieces

The | pig | is | in | the | box | .

Color these rectangle pieces light blue and cut them out for your puzzle pieces.

The | cat | is | in | the | box | .

Color these rectangle pieces pink and cut them out for your puzzle pieces.

The | dog | is | in | the | box | .

Color these rectangle pieces light green and cut them out for your puzzle pieces.

The | hat | is | in | the | box | .

Color these rectangle pieces light orange and cut them out for your puzzle pieces.

Spell it like you mean it. N

Color dashes blue	Color dashes pink
Color dashes green	Color dashes orange
Color dashes yellow	Color dashes purple

Puzzle pieces for initial letters worksheets

Aa	Ee	Ii	Oo	Uu
Aa	Ee	Ii	Oo	Uu
Mm	Ss	Ff	Tt	Hh
Dd	Jj	Vv	Nn	Kk
Bb	Ll	Pp	Ww	Cc
Rr	Yy	Zz	Gg	Qu qu

(For use with pages 54, 55, 56 and 57)

113

Puzzle pieces for vowel practice worksheet

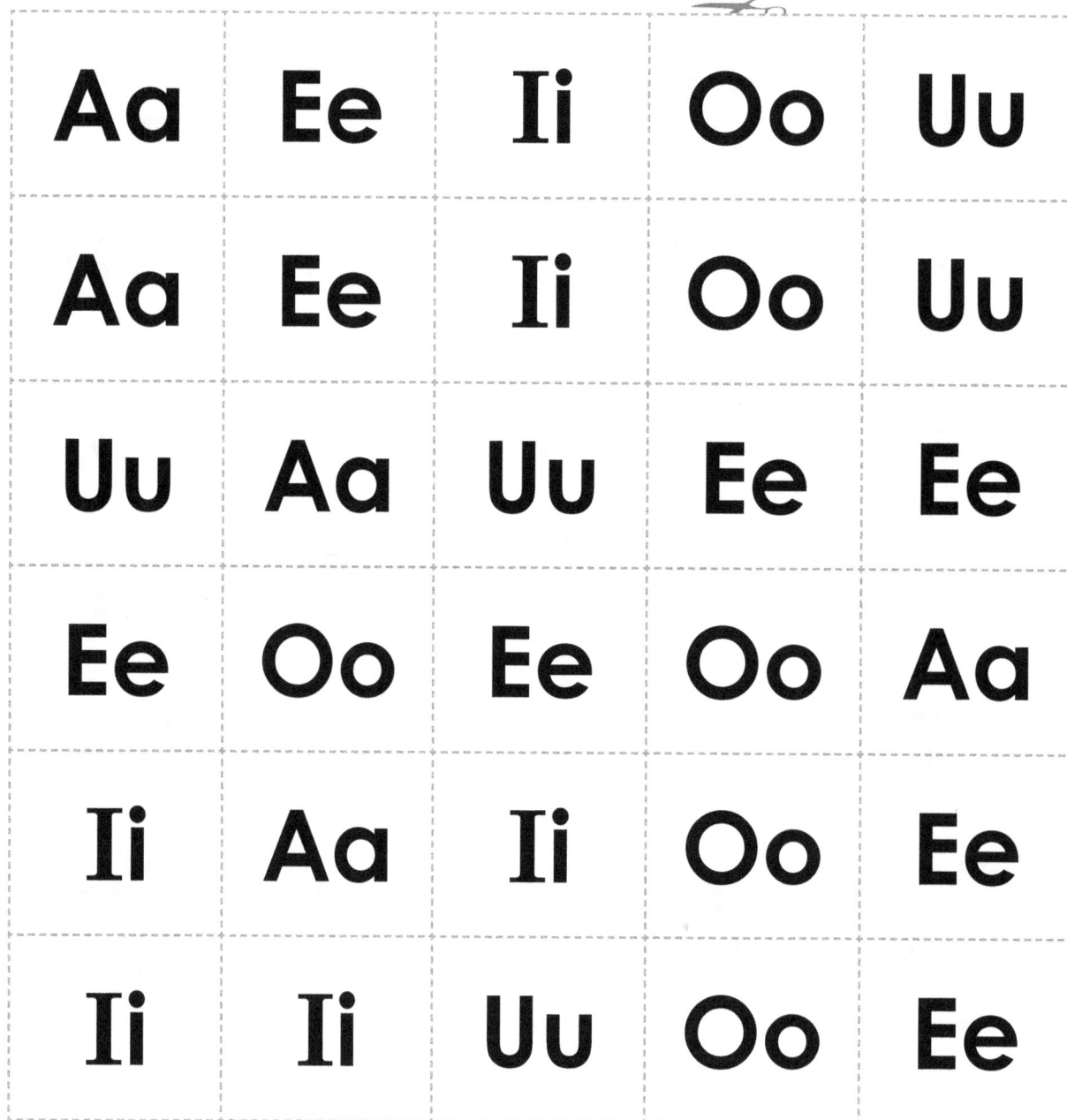

Aa	Ee	Ii	Oo	Uu
Aa	Ee	Ii	Oo	Uu
Uu	Aa	Uu	Ee	Ee
Ee	Oo	Ee	Oo	Aa
Ii	Aa	Ii	Oo	Ee
Ii	Ii	Uu	Oo	Ee

(For use with page 58)

Puzzle pieces for tricky consonant worksheet

Nn	Ll	Rr	Hh	Ll
Rr	Nn	Dd	Ll	Rr
Ll	Hh	Rr	Ll	Nn
Rr	Nn	Ll	Dd	Ll
Ll	Nn	Rr	Hh	Ll
Rr	Rr	Nn	Ll	Rr

(For use with page 59)

Puzzle pieces for blends worksheets

l	fl	cl	l	sl
pl	l	gl	bl	n
sn	t	st	str	r
fr	br	gr	r	pr
cr	tr	dr	sp	sm
tw	sc	sw	sk	dr

(For use with pages 63, 64)

116

Puzzle pieces for digraph worksheet

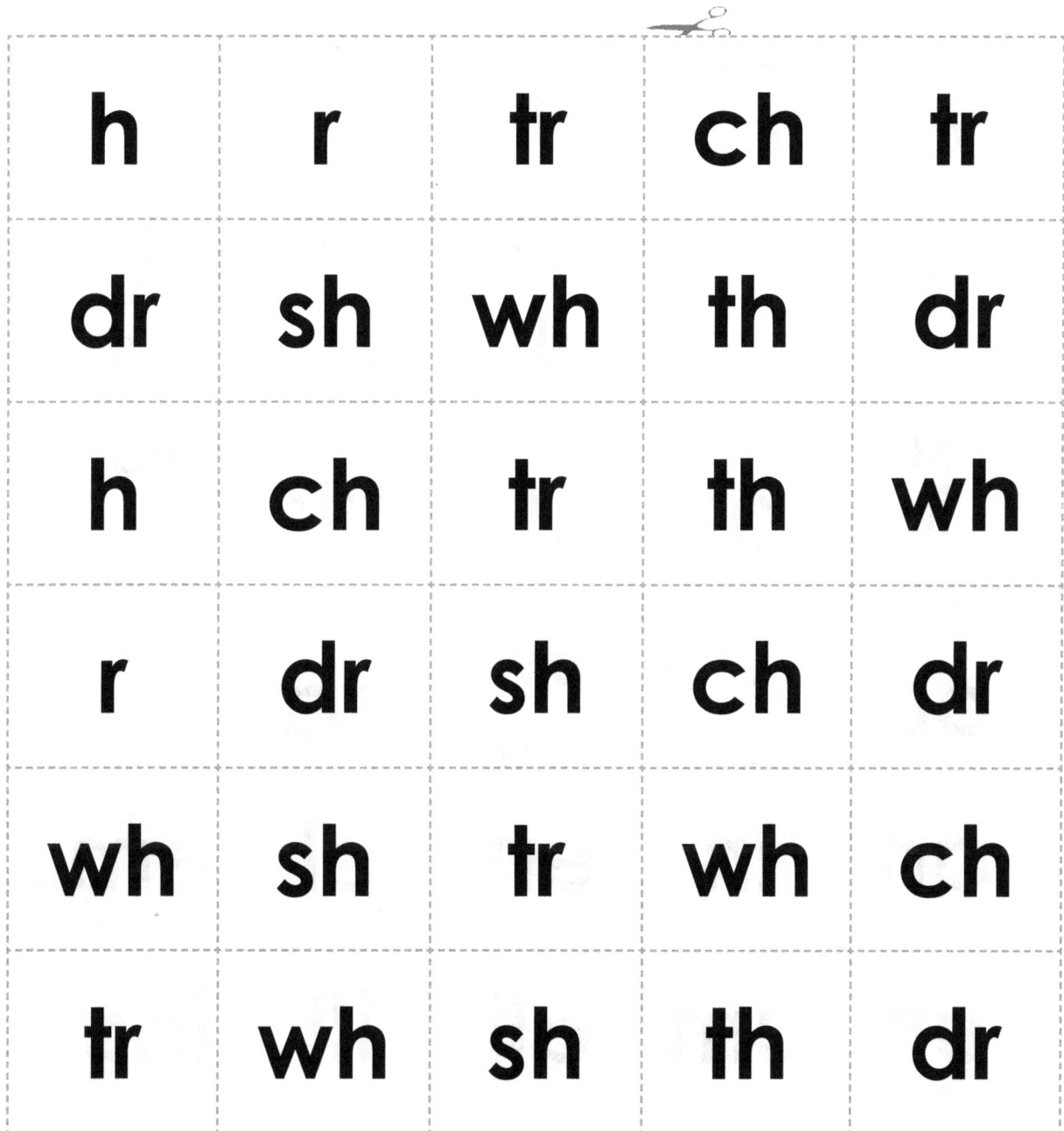

h	r	tr	ch	tr
dr	sh	wh	th	dr
h	ch	tr	th	wh
r	dr	sh	ch	dr
wh	sh	tr	wh	ch
tr	wh	sh	th	dr

(For use with page 67)

Puzzle pieces for digraphs/vowel sounds worksheets

a ay ai	e ee ea	i igh	o oa	U
sh	ch	th th	wh ph	c k ck
er ir ur	or	ar	air	ear eer
oo	oy oi	ow ou	ha	hi
an	in	en	el	em
un	um	all	ill	ing
a	e	i	i	o	u

(For use with page 68,69,70 and 71)

(Color the lines on p.75 to make the puzzle piece colors indicated here)

Color/Highlight letter pieces blue	Color/Highlight letter pieces pink
c g g c	kn kn mb mb

Color/Highlight letter pieces green	Color/Highlight letter pieces orange
er er ir ir ur ur	ed ed ed

Color/Highlight letter pieces yellow	
a a e	

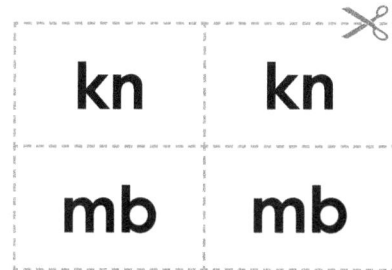

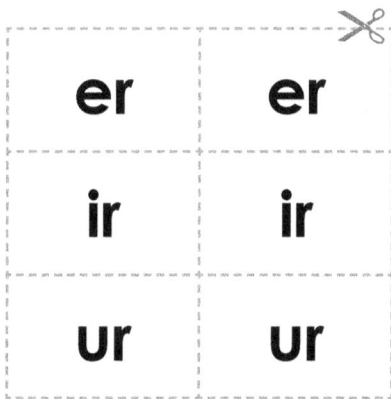

(For use with page 75)

119

(Color the lines on p.76-77 to make the puzzle piece colors indicated here)

Color/Highlight letter pieces blue	Color/Highlight letter pieces pink
who she him he her they them	what this that these those

Color/Highlight letter pieces green	Color/Highlight letter pieces orange
where there when then	why because

Color/Highlight letter pieces yellow	Color/Highlight letter pieces purple
We went swimming said the children .	I want to go for a walk said the dog .

(For use with page 76,77)

Puzzle N Pieces

(Color the lines on p.112 to make the puzzle piece colors indicated here)

Color/Highlight letter pieces blue

c	a	t
p	i	g
d	o	g
u	p	

Color/Highlight letter pieces pink

sh	ell
t	en
r	un
an	t

Color/Highlight letter pieces green

ch	ee	se
sh	ar	k
dr	e	ss
wh	a	le

Color/Highlight letter pieces orange

c	ow	
b	oa	t
f	ee	t
m	ai	l

Color/Highlight letter pieces yellow

c	ar	
s	t	ar
g	ir	l
h	or	se

Color/Highlight letter pieces purple

fl	ow	er	
l	igh	t	
n	um	b	er	s
sp	i	d	er

(For use with page 112)